GOD'S SHADOW

GOD'S SHADOW
Prison Poems

Reza Baraheni

Bloomington · Indiana University Press · London

Published in Canada by Fitzhenry & Whiteside Limited, Don Mills, Ontario

Manufactured in the United States of America

Library of Congress Cataloging in Publication Data
Baraheni, Reza, 1935–
  God's shadow.
  1. Political prisoners—Iran—Poetry. I. Title.
PK6561.B35A22   891'.55'13   75-34731
ISBN 0-253-13218-5   1 2 3 4 5 80 79 78 77 76

The book is dedicated to

Jalal Al-Ahmad, *friend, killed*
Samad Behrangi, *friend, killed*
Khosrow Golesorkhi, *friend, killed*
Karamat Daneshiyan, *killed*
and
The political prisoners of Iran
and
The imprisoned peoples of Iran

CONTENTS

CONTENTS

ACKNOWLEDGMENTS

My thanks, first and foremost, go to Paul Engle and Hualing Nieh Engle, whose generosity and capacity for human understanding made it possible for me to write these poems in the stimulating atmosphere of Iowa City. If I deserved *that* prison, I also deserved the company of the Engles as compensation. Their prodigious gifts, in the form of a nongovernmental grant, brought my family and me to the United States and provided for our stay while I completed these poems. All but two of them were written in Persian during my visit in the States.* "The Doves" and "The Light of Home" I wrote on prison walls with my fingernails, memorizing each stanza, erasing it so that I wouldn't get caught, and scratching the following stanzas in the same fashion until the whole poem was completed. My prison friends carried them in their memories to other prisons. One poem was in fact an earlier piece, to which I added lines reflecting the prison experience.

I translated the poems into English myself with considerable assistance from three friends who are themselves talented poets and writers. David St. John assisted in the translation of "An Epic in Reverse," "Cemetery," and "Ass Poem." Burt Blume assisted with "Nostalgia," "Crying," "Another Dream," "How Long Must the Game Last?" "Lamentation," "Ahmad Agha's Prison Dream," and "Broken Images of Decay." The remainder were translated with the aid of Michael Henderson. I thank each for his contribution of hours of labor. I am particularly grateful to Denise Levertov, whose valuable suggestions I appreciated and used. However, I accept full responsibility for the form and content of the English versions.

When I started to add the date on which I completed the introduction, I found to my surprise that it was on this very day last year that I was released from prison. I am grateful to all the American writers and poets who made my release possible. Their

---

*A Persian edition, published in 1976, is available from Abjad Publications, 853 Broadway, Suite 414, New York, N.Y. 10003.

efforts were led by Jerzy Kosinski, president of the American chapter of PEN, and eventually were taken up by my Iranian friends in CAIFI. I hope they will continue their efforts on behalf of other prisoners.

And finally, my thanks to George Novack, a generous father to all prisoners and to men and women under persecution everywhere.

My wife, Sanaz, I can thank personally. She made the world possible.

Reza Baraheni

December 22, 1974

Introduction

THE PISTOL IN THE HAND of the tall, bearded young man was aimed at me when I rolled down the car window at the stoplight at the end of Queen Elizabeth Boulevard. It was a dirty day, a dirty crossroad, and the dirtiest hour in the blazing sun of Teheran, and the man's face was no less dirty. But he was recklessly cool. When he lifted his dark glasses to his sweating forehead, he seemed oblivious to the cars honking from all directions and the bystanders gathering to watch.

"If you make a move, I'll blow your brains out," he said. He thrust his hand inside the car, opened the door, and sat beside me with the pistol pointed at my ribs. "Move on and stop on the other side."

"But who are you?" I asked as soon as I could speak, although I could already guess.

"I'm an agent of SAVAK,"* he mumbled, "and you have to come with us." The onlookers had disappeared, seeing the pistol, and the cars moved on as if nothing had happened. When I stopped my car on the other side of the light, we were joined by one of three people in a car parked ahead.

My wife and some other relatives were waiting for me at the top of the stairs when I went up with three secret police behind me. I winked at Sanaz, telling her, "We have guests."

"But why didn't you say so?" she protested. "I thought we

---

*The Iranian secret police.

were all going to eat out." The search of the house began right away while everyone watched. They knew what they were doing. In less than an hour everything in the apartment was heaped in the middle of the rooms. Even children's toys were torn open and inspected. The driver, who had identified himself as the leader, went through all the shelves of Persian books, picking one here and another there and putting them on the desk.

"Let's go," he said to me. I wanted to have time to think and, more important, to give my wife all the money I had with me.

"Are you sure I'm the guy you want?" I said. "There is another Dr. Baraheni besides me." They wouldn't bother to go after my older brother, who was a professor of psychology in the University of Teheran. He was a quiet man who had never spoken or written anything against the authorities. While the agent spoke into the walkie-talkie, I took the money out of my pocket and handed it to Sanaz.

"Your first name is Reza, isn't it?"

"Yes," I said.

He said something into the walkie-talkie again, then turned to me. "It's you we want. Let's go." Then he looked at my wife. "Madame," he said, "we'll bring the professor back in two hours." I didn't know yet that the two hours would stretch into 102 days.

After a drive of about an hour, during which I was blindfolded, we arrived at our destination in the center of the city. They took everything away from me. When they blindfolded me again, I had no belt, shoelaces, socks, handkerchief, pen, pencil, or paper. They also made a list of the books they had taken from my apartment and forced me to sign a letter which stated that those "dangerous books" belonged to me. I was led somewhere again and pushed through several iron doors, while being told, "Lift your foot up, put your foot down," as we went through them. The final one was opened with a pulling of bolts and a hammerlike sound. I was shoved in, the blindfold was removed, and I found myself in what I was later to learn was Dungeon No. 14.

I was still naïve enough to think that they couldn't do this to me, that they would come back any minute to apologize for what they had done. But the events that followed proved that, like my nation, I too had been taught to believe in miracles. They came again at about eight o'clock and took me out blindfolded and handcuffed. Again we passed through several iron doors, and finally, when they took the handkerchief away, I was facing a man who told me to sit down and answer his questions. Although he didn't inform me of specific charges against me, he accused me of having dealings with the Confederation of Iranian Students Abroad, which I denied. I had made no secret of my critical attitude toward the present government of Iran, however—had in fact published my views in books and articles* and had talked relatively openly, if not freely, with my colleagues and students at the university. From the lines that my interrogation took during those 102 days, it is clear that both my political and my literary views were what had aroused SAVAK's interest in me. And I don't doubt that the fact of my coming from a group that represents an ethnic minority in Iran further intensified their interest.†

During this first encounter with my accusers I was aware of all kinds of noises, people screaming and pleading for help, others swearing at the top of their voices; the sounds of whips and maces mingled with the moaning of men and women. Where was I? I actually had the nerve to ask.

---

*Masculine History, a book in which I discussed the causes of cultural disintegration in Iran, had appeared early in 1973. "The Culture of the Oppressor and the Culture of the Oppressed," an article dealing with the Iranian government's heavyhanded treatment of ethnic groups in Iran other than Persian, had come out in August 1973. Two other articles that described the history and the politics of the opposition in Iran had followed it. At the same time Events and Parents, a poem about the plight of the Turkish nationals in Iran, had appeared in Teheran Journal, an English daily. The prison interrogation, however, covered my whole literary career.

†Iran has a population of around 34 million, but only 14 to 16 million are Persian. There are 10 million Turks, 4 million Kurds, 2 million Arabs and Baluchis, and 2 million others in the north of the country who speak two dialects of an ancient Persian hardly understood by modern Persians. As a result of the government's decree that Persian be the official language of all nationalities in the country, sixty percent of the people cannot use their own languages. I come from Iran's Turkish nationality.

"None of your business, you son of a bitch," the man shouted. "We ask the questions here, not traitors like you!" There were all sorts of questions dealing with my life, but mostly focusing on the last twenty years, my literary career. Afterward, I was blindfolded and handcuffed again and taken back to the dungeon.

It was a four by eight foot hole illuminated only by the light admitted through a small window barred on both sides. Shouting came from all over the place, almost as if a great religious procession were moving along the corridors. The sound of whispering came from the other cells. Sometimes there would be loud moaning or sobbing, and generally when the iron door of the ward was opened and shut, there would be wailing and crying. Nothing but prison sounds could be heard. The next night I would join the ranks of the underground wailers and mourners. I put my jacket under my head as a pillow and tried in vain to go to sleep. In less than six hours I had been disconnected from the rest of the world.

I believe I had just closed my eyes when suddenly the door was flung open with a bang that sent me up from the floor to the door. It was morning. I hadn't realized it. Days come and go in prison without the prisoner becoming conscious of the light of day. A new guard was standing in front of me with the blindfold hanging from his shoulder.

"Get up," he said, "and put on your shoes." From behind the blindfold I could realize the faint light of the sun. When I was being taken through the courtyard, I heard somebody shout, "Bring that son of a bitch here!" I was pushed into a room and the blindfold was removed. There was a group of people in suits and ties, and several others in sweaters, and several more with blindfolds and handcuffs. This last group couldn't stand properly. They seemed to be suffering from something in their shoulders, legs, feet, heads, and hands.

My first "interrogation" took the form of a tirade delivered with kicks and blows by a well-dressed, bald man with very red eyes. He gave me no opportunity to explain anything, but it was clear that he didn't like my origins, my profession, and my writings, not to mention my beard. When he tired of the slapping and kicking, he turned to the guard who had brought me to him: "Go get someone to shave his beard." The man who arrived was the prison medic and was called "Doctor" by the prisoners. A pitiless man, he wouldn't even give them aspirin. He had no razor with him to shave me, but the bald man wouldn't take no for an answer. He slapped me a couple more times and ordered the medic to shave me with his scissors. The man took a pair of surgery scissors from his sack, led me to the side of the water pool in the middle of the yard, sat me down, and started cutting my beard. Whenever his tiny scissors were not a match for my long, thick beard, he would virtually pull the hair out very roughly with the ends of the scissors. Then I heard the bald man shout from the room, "Take the bastard into *Otagh-e Tamshiyat!*" I had never before heard this combination of words, half Turkish and half Arabic. Literally the phrase means "the room in which you make people walk," but I soon found out that it actually meant the torture chamber. I was blindfolded again and led by two of the guards, one on each side, up a long flight of stairs to the infamous third floor. When the order to take off the blindfold came, I found myself in the midst of four men besides the guards. I wondered what they were going to do to me. They called each other "Doctor"—Dr. Azudi, Dr. Hosseini, and so on. It was only later that I came to realize that by using a university title, they provided themselves, rather unconsciously, with a certain legitimacy to deal with university students and teachers like myself.

"Tie him up," Dr. Azudi ordered his men, and turning to me he said, "Go lie down." There was a bed on the floor. There were also two other iron beds, one on top of the other, in another corner of the room. These last two, I later learned, were used to burn the backs, generally the buttocks, of prisoners. They tie you on your back to the upper bed, and with the heat coming from a torch or a small heater, they burn your back to get the information they want. Sometimes the burning is concentrated on the spine, and paralysis nearly always follows. There were all sizes of whips hanging from nails on the walls. Electric batons stood on little stools, and a nail plucking instrument as well. The gallows on the other side was used to hang you upside down; then someone

[15]

would beat you with a mace on your legs, or use the electric baton on your chest or on your genitals. Or they would lower you down, pull your pants up, and one of them try to rape you.

In the other torture rooms were worse instruments that other prisoners would describe: the weight-cuffs that break your shoulders in less than two hours; the electric shock instrument, apparently a recent introduction into the Iranian torture industry; and the pressure device, which applies pressure on the skull until you either tell them what they want or hear your bones break into pieces.

The more horrible instruments were kept on the second floor, where I was not taken, but the office of my interrogator, Rezvan, was next to this chamber, and one day when he was called to another office for some sort of consultation, I walked into this chamber and looked around. It resembles an ancient Egyptian tomb and is reserved for those persons suspected of being terrorists or accused of having made attempts on the life of the Shah or the members of the royal family.*

I lay down on my stomach but was immediately ordered by Azudi to lie on my back. My hands and feet were tied to the two ends of the bed by the guards. Azudi sat by me on the bed. I didn't know his name until later when I described him to the other prisoners, who added that he was the head torturer, feared even by the other torturers. He was responsible only to the bald man, who later identified himself as Hosseinzadeh and told me

---

*The general pattern for the administration of torture in the prison, as pieced together from my personal experiences and observations and from conversations with other prisoners, is as follows. Initially the prisoner is beaten, often by several men at once using sticks. If the beating fails to produce a confession, he may be hung upside down, beaten again, and even raped. If he continues to resist, electric shocks are administered. In some instances teeth are pulled out, a hot iron rod is thrust through the cheek until it sears the mouth and tongue, or—in extreme cases—boiling water may be pumped into the victim's rectum, or a heavy weight suspended from his testicles. In the case of women prisoners an electrified rod is commonly applied to the naked body, and the voltage increased as the rod is applied to the breasts and the vagina. Rape is a common practice. I have personal knowledge of an instance in which a thirteen-year-old girl was raped in the prison, and another in which a child of five or six was beaten for unwillingness to give information concerning a relative.

that he had been a student of mine and had received a D from me.

Azudi started beating me hard around my mouth, saying, "Tell me." I had forgotten the names of friends, writers, publishers, printers, and others whom I had taken into my confidence about my books and articles.

"What should I tell you?" I asked him.

"We know everything, but we want you to tell us everything yourself!"

"But I don't know anything! Ask me specific questions and I'll tell you everything!"

"I'll beat the shit out of you, if you don't tell me yourself!" he said. Then he took hold of the lower parts of my ribs and started to squeeze whatever internal organ he was holding in his hand. Was it my stomach, liver, kidney, or perhaps my heart he was holding? I have never been able to understand the human body properly, but at that moment I thought he was holding my whole life in his hand.

"I've done nothing! I've done nothing! I've got nothing to tell you," I mumbled.

"Yes, you have and you'll tell us!" grumbled Azudi, and then without turning his head to the others he said, "Parvizkhan, go ahead!" The flagellation started right away. It was a thick interwoven whip, made of wire with a knot at the end of it. The whip would go up, turn round the man's head, and descend with a whacking sound right on the soles of my feet. The man was a professional. He never missed. When the whip came down, it was like a huge hot charcoal, live, burning and tearing at the soles of the feet, crippling my whole legs. I was screaming at the top of my voice. Now I knew the meaning of the screams of the others the night before. These screams stayed with me for 102 days and when I left the prison, they didn't leave me.

The flagellation went on for some time, then Azudi called out to the man to stop, and when he did, Azudi placed his large iron fist on my cheek: "Tell us, if you don't want to die! Tell us!"

My feet were burning with pain: "Why don't you believe it? I don't have anything to tell you. If I had anything, I would tell you." He got up, grabbed the whip from the other man and started flagellating me all over. I started screaming again. He was so furious that he seemed angry at his own task.

"You son of a bitch, do you think I'll be satisfied with the kind of lies you're giving me! I've killed more than a hundred men on this bed." He got tired and he threw the whip to the other man, who caught it in midair and immediately started to work on my feet again. Flagellation is a kind of ever-present torture. Every interrogator carries a whip in his hand when he walks around in the prison or forces confessions.

Azudi came back and sat down. He told the man who was standing above my head, "Go ahead!" The man immediately began flagellating me on my hands. This whip was smaller and was made of leather rather than wire. But it wasn't flat. It really hurt. I could hear my own screams reflected from the prison walls. The voices of other prisoners and mine intermingled, forming something like a chorus for an Iranian Passion Play. Azudi's favorite parts of the human body seemed to be jaws and ribs. Struggling under his renewed blows, I managed to get one of my feet out of the rope. The beating stopped when that interrupted the ritual. The guard put my foot back into the noose and my adversaries continued their brutality until I fainted. I was out of breath from screaming and apparently they had also gotten a little tired, because when I regained consciousness, the whipper was wiping away his sweat and Azudi was sitting on one of the stools watching me.

He came and sat by me on the bed. He put his thick and fleshy hand on my cheek and patted me like a child. There was something sexual in the way he did this. Then he raised his hand as high as he could and slapped me on the same cheek: "Listen, you son of a bitch! We have the tape of your speech in the States against the Shah, we have all the things you said against the White Revolution,* and now we have a written document in the

---

*The Shah's "reform" movement, initiated in January 1963, and amended several times during the last twelve years. Any conversation or written material on the failures of the "White Revolution" leads to immediate incarceration and torture.

paper. We have all your books too, proof that your intention is to overthrow the rule of the Shah. You're a traitor, and you know what we do with traitors? We fuck them first and then we kill them."

"But why don't you bring me to trial?" I said, "Don't you think that if you have all these documents against me, ou cany easily lock me up?"

"This *is* the court. There is no other court. I'm the judge, the jury, the court, and the executioner. You know what they call me here? Tell him, Parvizkhan!"

"The Executioner for His Imperial Majesty the Shahanshah, the Light of the Aryans."

Then Azudi added, "I'll pull your tongue out of your mouth and I'll break your fingers one by one, so that you won't be able to say anything or write anything." Saying this, he took the smallest finger of my left hand and broke it. I started screaming and the flagellation began again and continued until I fainted. When I woke again, Azudi was still sitting by me. There were now two whippers, one on either side.

"Are you married?" Azudi asked.

"Yes," I said.

"Is your wife an American?"

"No, she isn't," I said.

"Is she an Iranian?"

"Yes," I said.

"Then I'll have her brought here and I'll have the guards fuck her right in front of your eyes."

I had heard stories of that, but I never knew that I might have to confront it one day. I didn't know what to say. I looked away.

"You have a daughter, don't you?" he asked.

"Yes."

"How old is she?"

"Thirteen."

"How nice. Guard? How would you like to fuck a girl of thirteen?"

The guard didn't say anything. The torturers laughed.

"Are you going to tell us now?"

"But why don't you understand? I've got nothing to tell you!"

"Are you going to tell us who told you to write that article?"

I knew he meant the article I had written about twenty days earlier, "The Culture of the Oppressor and the Culture of the Oppressed." I had tried to analyze the oppressive nature of the government's cultural policies, and the article had been interpreted as an attack on the Shah's attitude toward the peasants and the workers and on his racist policies in relation to the plight of large and small minorities in Iran.

But I asked, "Which article do you mean?"

"The one in which you say something about the Turks in Iran!"

"No, I wrote that article by myself. I write all my articles myself."

"Did anyone see the article before it was published?"

I had read it to several friends, and several others had asked me to write my opinion on the present cultural situation, and there were a few friends in the press who had given me encouragement, but I couldn't possibly say anything about these people. I would not disclose their names even now.

"No, nobody saw it before I published it in the paper. But the censors in the Ministry of Information must have seen it before it got published."

He knew that I was blaming the government censorship for the publication of the article. They started again, two people flagellating this time. When one of the whips was up, the other was on the soles of my feet. I was screaming again, but not with the same energy. Azudi got up himself and took another whip and joined in. Then, hysterically, he suddenly grabbed my sides and tried to raise me on my feet, but he couldn't. The guards and the others helped him by untying me from the bed. Azudi lifted me up and pushed me to the corner of the room: "You bastard! I'm going to kill you this very minute!" I couldn't stand on my feet and I fell down. He lifted me up again and then took a pistol out of his belt. He put it to my temple. The other torturers started

kicking me and shouting, "Behave yourself! Stand up straight!"
The pistol against my temple gave me the shock of my life. Still,
almost by instinct, I thought I should do something to save my-
self. He took the pistol away, loaded it, and held it back at my
temple. I had almost forgotten the pain in my hands and feet,
my mouth, ribs, and insides. I was sweating all over. Was I also
pissing? "Tell me!" He was using all the obscenities he could
think of. I had contracted my face, waiting for a miracle to save
me. I must have looked ridiculous because the others were laugh-
ing. Then the trigger was pulled, or so I felt, and I fell down with
my head blown off. My head knew that it was blown off. When I
gained consciousness again, I was being carried down on the back
of a guard. Later, one of the guards told me that one of the tor-
turers had imitated the sound of shooting with his mouth and
hands before I fainted.

In only a few hours the torture chamber takes you to your
origins, with fear as the only monarch. The meaning of life eludes
you, and you are hung in a stupid void in which you are totally
and desperately alone.

The torture does not end the first day or the first week, even
if it may cease for a while. Rather, it becomes deeply psychologi-
cal as time goes on. You are taken out to be shot and you are not.
But it takes you two hours of absolute terror to realize that. And
then this very action begins to have such an awesome reality
in your mind that later, even after you are released, it becomes
part of your maimed subconscious, as if you had inherited it
from a genetically subhuman ancestor and you could do nothing
about it.

This is not the place for a detailed account of my life in
prison. The full story will be told elsewhere.* But I would like
the reader of these poems to be aware of the circumstances that
led me to write them, for they arose out of real life in the most
brutal way, and I wrote them in the hope that they will offer new
insights as well as with the hope that they will be enjoyed as

---

*I have written a full account of my prison days in Persian, but it has not
been published yet.

poems. I call them poems of factuality, for they are concerned with genuine experience—not things that I imagined, not abstract or ideological matters. I could have thought about the painful and dehumanizing events that lie at the heart of these poems before going to prison; but I could not have written about them in the same way.

The kind of hell embodied in the prison life briefly described here is simply the product of the power that some people hold over others—in the case of contemporary Iran, power held by a relatively small group over a vast population, which the regime would like to expand to include the Arabs, the Afghans, the Pakistanis, and the whole of the Persian Gulf and the Indian Ocean. That such a prison as "The Joint Committee of the Campaign against Terrorism in Iran" could exist and that such extra-legal incarceration could take place betray the values of the people in power. One writes about these things partly in the hope, in reality an impossible hope, of exorcising what one has actually experienced, and in the last analysis, one writes in the hope that people will hear, believe, and draw back in repulsion from a system in which such things could take place.

The Iranian spirit, having suffered centuries of oppression under a most brutal structure of monarchy, which I have called Masculine History, is degenerating under the kind of fascism introduced by the present regime: Aryanomania; anti-Semitism; strict Persian nationalism—which means the suppression of other nationalities in Iran; the militarization of the country—Iran has a military budget higher than any in the whole history of the Middle East and higher than all the funds used for other purposes combined; the use of censorship by SAVAK—not one newspaper in Iran criticizes the system; the existence of more than half a million secret police and an equal number of informants; and the bureaucratization of the whole system and the suppression of all opposition in the country.

Several prison incidents were, nevertheless, a source of unique joy to me. They all reveal the significance of poetry in the lives of the Iranians, and they help to reclaim for poetry the position it once held both in primitive times and in the Classical period of Persian literature.

Prisoners may pray, swear, or keep silent before torture; they may scream, weep, or stay quiet during torture; but almost without exception they recite poetry after torture. The Iranian mind, beating to the rhythm of musical words, is a great reservoir of images strung to short and long lines of modern poetry. The prisoner doesn't consider this poetry something very personal; he thinks of it as collective lines of words imbued with collective fears and hopes. Sometimes a newly tortured man would start to recite the first few lines of a poem and then it would be picked up by someone else in another cell, turning gradually into a muffled chorus of pain and pleasure within the four walls of the ward. A poet is immediately recognized in prison, even by the guards, whose minds still retain something of their original innocence.

On the third day of my imprisonment I kept calling the guard to come and open the door and let me go to the toilet. The ward was comparatively silent and I could hear my own voice reflected in the other cells. The guard was not there. Perhaps he had locked the ward door and gone away on some errand, but I still kept calling him, thinking that he was there and just not bothering to respond. After almost an hour I gave up and fell silent. Then I suddenly heard a voice familiar as my own, reciting something that seemed too intimate for me not to recognize as a dream of mine. The tortured voice had risen from the other side of the ward, had lost all timidity, and was reciting a poem I had written almost ten years ago, repressed because of its political allusions. Later, on a Friday afternoon when we were standing blindfolded in the line for the prison showers, someone whispered a few words to me identifying himself as the one who had recited the poem. I didn't know who he was, and I still don't, but he turned that poem into a prison chorus.

The second incident also shines as a bright moment for poetry. Seyyed Ali was a poet with whom I shared a cell for almost fifteen days. We would recite poems to each other almost daily, and sometimes even the guards would open the door and sit down and listen. There was a guard whose parents were Turkish and Kurdish who had been given strict orders not to talk to me and not to approach my cell because of my ideas on the rights of minorities in Iran. He called me Uncle Poet when there was nobody watching him, and I could see that he was looking for an opportunity to talk to me. He got it on a cold December night when he was posted as the only ward guard. He opened the door very quietly and beckoned me to come out and follow him. He had closed all the holes on the doors of the other cells. We went to the toilet. He closed the door and then he said, "Uncle, let me hear a poem." I recited not one but several poems to him. Sometimes he would interrupt and ask me for the meaning of a line here or a word there, and finally he asked me to dictate a short piece, which he seemed to like very much, and he took it down in his rather clumsy handwriting. Finally we kissed each other, almost in tears. We had forgotten where we were. The toilet and the ward in the background did not count. He rushed me to my cell as soon as he heard a noise from the ward door and locked me in. That guard cannot be a butcher, and only those who do not listen to the voice of poetry have the capacity to become butchers.

I was released from the prison on December 22, 1973, 102 days after I had been taken there for "a couple of hours." The release came as abruptly as the imprisonment had. There can be no doubt that it came about only as the result of the efforts of a group of writers in Europe and America.

On the fourth day after my release, my friends sent me from a provincial town in Iran some parts of documents, which were later made fully available to me by the Committee for Artistic and Intellectual Freedom in Iran (CAIFI). The letter that had been so instrumental in my release was the following one published in the *New York Times*, Sunday, December 16, 1973. It was signed by three distinguished American writers and artists representing thirty-five others. I was released a week after it appeared.

A Poet in Jail

To the Editor:

In September 1973, Reza Baraheni, prominent poet and literary critic, was arrested and imprisoned by the Iranian government after his return to Iran from a year's teaching at American universities in Texas and Utah. Mr. Baraheni was released shortly afterward and resumed his writing but was almost immediately rearrested.*

Although Iranian newspapers have not yet reported his imprisonment, Mr. Baraheni, who is a professor at the University of Teheran, has remained in prison now for more than two months. His hair and beard were shaved off and there are indications that he has been tortured.

Little of his writing is yet available in the West, but Mr. Baraheni is the author of twenty books. He is the founder of modern literary criticism in Persian. He is a journalist, poet, novelist, playwright and scholar. Indeed, Mr. Baraheni is Iran's Solzhenitsyn†—outspoken and fiercely independent.

As writers, scholars and individuals concerned with the right of free expression everywhere, we protest against the Iranian government's harassment and imprisonment of one of the country's leading authors. We believe that in the light of the close diplomatic and military relationships between the United States and Iranian Governments, it is especially important for Americans to speak out in defense of Reza Baraheni.

We call upon the Iranian authorities to release him forthwith from prison, restore his full rights and liberties and permit him to resume his academic and literary functions.

New York, December 12, 1973

JERZY KOSINSKI
JOSEPH HELLER
DWIGHT MACDONALD

---

*I was arrested only once, but the mistake is understandable in view of the fact that the Iranian government releases no information on its prisoners.

†Mr. Solzhenitsyn is certainly a very great writer, but as soon as he tries to expound his political ideology and historical theory, he becomes so reactionary that I am hard-pressed to find any similarity between my "independence" and his.

[25]

The response to this letter by the Iranian Embassy was so brutal that it could almost have been the writing of Azudi.

Guilty in Iran

To the Editor:
  In your issue of December 16, you published a letter entitled "Poet in Jail." Regarding this letter, I would like to point out that in Iran, as in any other nation, a person who is found guilty of a crime by the courts or who is found to threaten the security of a nation is treated in a manner that he will no longer be a threat to or continue to disrupt the society in which he lives.

Washington, Dec. 20, 1973

NASSER SHIRZAD
Press Counselor,
Embassy of Iran

After my release, although I resumed teaching, I could only circulate under the constant surveillance of the secret police. My movements were restricted, and above all there was no hope of my being able to publish within my native country anything that honestly expressed my thoughts. These poems could not have appeared in Iran. It is my hope that that very fact will make them, if not better poems, more meaningful ones for the reader who picks up this book.

Unlike previous works of mine and current publications by other Iranian writers, this volume of poetry was written without the interfering editorial hand of SAVAK. I believe it is the first of its kind in contemporary Persian literature in light of the fact that all my other books and those of my friends were checked and changed by SAVAK before publication. For the first time I feel responsible for a book of my own.

GOD'S SHADOW

AN EPIC IN REVERSE
. . . .

We have reached the end of the road we had chosen
A tall tree with
all its intricate nests has fallen
When
we look at the ditches and trenches
we see the heads of birds
the thin arms of ghetto children
   severed from their lean bodies
and half-burned books which
the rain has kept from burning entirely

From train stations
the smell of wet tobacco opium and insomnia
came
and the imprisoned air of centuries
The rush of the crowd and
the steady falling of feet on the dust-covered floors
spoke
of a criminal lunacy
In the next moment the faces of departure rose behind
   the windows
as if the travelers as well as those seeing them off knew
all would be dumped in waterless deserts
The train took a retired nation with
its chain of rotten images to the salt steppes
and the consumption of a poisonous tradition
ate at the lungs like a distracted hyena

We continued on our way
In the middle of the road we saw distraught poets
throwing their words at indifferent soldiers
—like lunatics tossing flowers at this man or that man—
and the soldiers stood at attention like slender, metallic pricks
so that

the Shah and the Queen and their ministers would come and pass
We continued on our way because
we had to reach the end of the road we had chosen
And passing we saw our Father
among the crowd with two wide-open mouths
his blue eyes fixed on the royal route of the Shah and the Queen
We said, Father come with us
He opened his mouth
to speak but
one mouth swallowed the words of the other
and Father's voice could not be heard
The wind blew down the street like the germs of rabies
flying the Shah and the Queen as its retinue
They were two tall vultures who
had found young corpses
and had to pierce them with their beaks
The dogs in the square synchronized their steps with
the heavy beat of the military march and
rabid cats applauded
Father raised his hands to the sky
praying and
the wind was shaking the sun behind the silk of the sky
Mother had unveiled herself and was trying to speak Turkish[1]
but her words were incomprehensible as if she'd discovered
the alphabet of an ancient language and
only by screaming could announce it to the world
The crowd was trampling
each other's shoulders breasts and hands
The whinny of horses the sound of cars and human voices mixed
The buildings all stood tilted
Had an earthquake turned the world upside down for a second?
Had the camera thrust in one's mind the image of an
    accidental moment?
My brother and I lifted
the shrouded body of our Father, one of us on either side
and slowly
we lowered the body into the deep graves of Vadiyossalam[2]

—Will Father's feet grow from the other side of the hemisphere
perhaps a bright hemisphere?—
Mother had put on her veil and
was begging in Turkish in the royal road of the Shah
    and the Queen
And we were passing because
we had to reach the end of the road we had chosen

The pictures of the Shah and the Queen
were smiling witnesses of the tattered rooms of New City[3]
Pimps got their tips under those pictures
and when one was left alone with a whore
his mind would be so excited that it seemed
everything in the room
—from the mattress on the floor to the windows covered
    with newspaper—
had been invisibly electrified
and thinking about those things
would turn one's brain cells to ashes
There we were reminded of
the times our Mother took us out of the city, away
    from everyone,
    to graze
We would graze our lunch from the earth
A few steps away
sheep cows and donkeys grazed
We on our stomachs and they on all fours
Older brother imitated the cows chewing their cud
We imitated our brother and
an hour later the pincers of scorpions started in our stomach
and our vomit smelled of newly plowed, fertilized earth
Dead ants floated in the bile and watery blood

On our way we saw rusted pistols of the Constitutional
    Revolution[4]
hanging on the walls of streets
Behind bookstore windows

Chekhov's picture with glasses
The wide beard and haggard eyes of a 70-year-old Tolstoy
and Mayakovsky's newly shaven head
    one day before his suicide
Hemingway's white beard
and Faulkner's alcoholic gaze
Mother would look at these pictures, holding a beggar's bowl
and say in Turkish
"None of these look like our men"[5]
My brother was telling passers-by in Persian
"Pity this poor woman,
her husband has just died and she's delirious"
And my sister gathered the small yellow coins
falling on the ground like the dry leaves of late autumn
And we continued on our way because
we had to reach the end of the road we had chosen

The bazaars looked like the Justice Department Morgue
The dead in rows on this side and that side
the only difference that the dead here traded with each other
Suddenly one of the dead would jump from a corner
—like a saint slipped away from a Byzantine mosaic—
and say, "Buy"
And our young pockets were too empty
for any thought of buying to sneak out of them
We'd leave the useless intricate tumult
the dead tumult of the bazaars,
like the cancered corpse of our father, behind
We'd walk madly up the Sepah Square
run deliriously the Shah and Shahreza avenues
and reach a place where
contractors engineers and commissioners
—this huge column of our enemies—
were drinking vodka
and with bloody fingers pulling the kabob
off burning skewers
The saliva would run so much in our mouths

that it would drop like sulphur out of our assholes
Out of hunger
even our pricks
rose big as the seed of a Persian date
    asking for food
We would wait in front of the wine houses
for the scraps to be dumped in the garbage
then dive headfirst into the trash cans
so like starving dogs only our feet showed
Pulled out we smelled like corpses
just yanked out of debris
Our faces resembled Breughel's beggars
and when we looked at our mother
she would be sitting at a corner of the street
We would unveil her
and see the female Buddha
who wept for the poverty of her sons
We would take her hand lift her up and
continue on our way because
we had to reach the end of the road we had chosen

The Shah is holding the oil in his hand like a glass of wine
drinking to the health of the West
and the Queen with her thick lips milks the tits of
    Motherland's doe
at night under the stars
in the day in the passage of sun
every month every year
And a glove the color of blood remains on the snows of
    St. Moritz
We look at the skiing pictures of the Shah on the snow
In the next picture
the Crown Prince walks down the airplane stairs
He passes the row of sixteen 50-year-old bald men
their heads thrust so far forward that
the Crown Prince seems to approve their total baldness
He gets in the helicopter

We hear its sound
and we think of widowed gardens and orphaned trees
and stone lying after stone
and league after league of deserts where
horses go mad of the heat
their last neighs coming down like swords
—striking nothing—
and wasted in the desert
We think of rifles with
sand stuck in their bolts
Of radiators with holes in them
in a heat 50 degrees above centigrade
and of staying staying staying
Of getting off the horses the mules and the cars
and throwing the rifles on the sands
and delivering the horses and the mules to the desert vultures
We see the Sphinx of mirage in front of us
and we think of that first promise
moving moving moving

Army barracks
have stretched their shit in the sun
The shit in universities is worse because
it's settled in the minds of professors
and turned to concrete
Our hope was not there
We went mad
and wrote with shaky hands
our messages on the walls of university toilets
away from the eyes of Abulgasemi[6]—the inborn hyena
    of the savak[7]
What could we do beyond this
We had to continue on our way
Reach the end of the road we had chosen

Death was a lighthouse approaching through the facing mist
We were the chosen men of death

And death was so bright in front of us that it seemed
a white horse was shining from the background of the dark
At night we'd sit together
like small innocent beasts
and make plans one after another almost from instinct
The hope of victory let
the rabbit of sleep into the ancient nest of eyes
and then we'd suddenly awake
with the breaking of the door falling of ladder opening of window
   the scattering of books the shining of weapons
and in the car a hand put the black blindfold on our eyes
A lake of cold sweat
   —fear—
drowned us
We would be driven to the dungeons
then to the torture chambers
and even there continued with our walking

Now this is the end of the road
The end of our conspiracies
The end of our history
The end of the epic of being, no!
   our not being
The end of our epic in reverse

The female Buddha
has put on her veil
on the road to the Chitgar firing range[8]
and in the dawn of the field
waits for us

And we have reached the end of the road we had chosen

THE DOVES

. . . .

outside doves perch everywhere
it is clear from
their cooings of love and delight
it is clear from
the whirr of their wings
wings which seem to fan me in my prisoner's sleep
it is clear outside
doves perch everywhere

the night is like a day on the other side of the bars
on this side the day is like the night

THE LIGHT OF HOME
. . . .

the sun has set
and the kite drifting
still glides above alien houses and nests
(take me back home!
take me back home!)

you have seen how a fish
out of water slaps the air in vain
you have seen how
(take me back home!
take me back home!)

you have seen how a horse,
broken-legged, gasps on the ground
you have seen how
(take me back home!)
take me back home!)

you have seen how night arrives
a tide of darkness nakedly engulfing
you have seen how
(take me back home!)

you have seen how a whiplash
cuts naked flesh like a sword
you have seen how

you have seen how a thousand nails
are pulled from their beds of flesh
how fingers and toes become beheaded martyrs
you have seen how
(take me back home!
take me back home!)

why is my tribe hidden behind a veil?
why for centuries have bloodthirsty generals
beaten their cymbals and drums in the name of my tribe?
why is wandering ever an addiction for my tribe?
what is it that, like a nightmare, has constricted
the breast of my tribe, its foul grip
keeping it on the floor of the sea for all eternity[1]
why is my tribe hidden behind a veil?
where is my tribe?
where is my tribe?

where is home?
home suggests the concrete in the lower depths
home is the correlative of chains blood
prison   home is torture from coast to coast
home is dawn executions death and martyrdom

the light of my home is not the light of prison
where is the light of home?
this is not the light of home
the door which is closed can also be opened
this is not the light of home
take me back home!
take me back home!

THE CRAZY DREAM OF THE PRISONER

. . . .

her eyes are larger than that
and the tip of her nose is uplifted more
and her lips
  are virgin pure
and her ears
  are like two tulips
    growing from the side of the moon

Mr. Picasso!
now that you've appeared in my dream
go ahead and paint, if you can!
use whichever period of yours you wish!

the wife of a prisoner is far more beautiful than that,
  Mr. Picasso!
especially when the prisoner doesn't know that after this
  sweet dream in the chamber where prisoners walk[1]
    Azudi and Hosseini and Parvizkhan[2]
      will stand over his head

DOCTOR AZUDI, THE PROFESSIONAL[1]

· · · · · · · · · · · ·

Azudi is just like
Genghis Khan   when he walks
he walks on a pile of fresh corpses

the Khan did not clean his teeth either
the Khan also belched   the Khan
did not take off his boots either   Azudi
has shattered the mouths of twenty poets today

Azudi wears a tie   something
Genghis Khan never did
only this splendid detail reveals the prodigious march of history

ZADAN! NAZADAN!¹

. . . .

suddenly a woman is sleepless in her dream
she screams:
   Nazan! Nazan! Nazan!
prisoners wake in the block one by one
and man and woman scream:
   Nazan! Nazan! Nazan!
and in the torture chambers
the beating begins
   Nazan! Nazan! Nazan!

THE DEATH OF THE POET
· · · · · · · · · · · · · · · ·

you have killed Khosrow Golesorkhi[1]
while the papers only boast your glories
while Mr. Georges Pompidou is also a poet
and the cadaver Queen of Iran has been elected to
honorary membership of the academy of old rabbits in France
we know that you have killed a poet called Khosrow Golesorkhi

we too have spies among the policemen
the sergeants and the agents of the SAVAK
——you have killed Khosrow Golesorkhi
this has nothing to do with your glories in the Iranian press
nothing to do with oil your money and the royal entourage aloft
on the shoulders of the SAVAK priests
nothing to do with the raven-pattern silk
woven by the hungry Baluch[2] laborers to cover
the symmetrical carcass of the Queen
nothing has anything to do with nothing
but the news of the shooting is everywhere
without the news of the shooting being anywhere
which confirms only one thing
you have killed Khosrow Golesorkhi

(perhaps one of the army companies which grew beards for three
months so they could parade the mask of Iran's divinity in front
of the Shah for ten minutes at the International Airport has
told us, or maybe a sheriff, after fruitlessly looking for a
guerrilla, has told his wife and she has told my wife and my
wife has rushed to the Statue Square and, screaming, told
everyone. perhaps perhaps perhaps. perhaps Dr. Azudi has told
me, professionally)

you have killed Khosrow Golesorkhi
because within four days you have opened a
  Mowlavi Foundation[3]

and four months ago you opened the Congress of Poetry
and *the Shah of Iran is counted among the great Iranian writers*
(so says Dr. Khanlari,[4] stillborn nanny to the adulterous
   sperm of
the Shah and the Queen—not me!)

you have killed Khosrow Golesorkhi
even before you killed him
you had killed him
you killed him two thousand five hundred years ago

THE POET

· · · · · · ·

our world survives on
two things   first
the poet and second the poet
and you have killed both
first: Khosrow Golesorkhi
second: Khosrow Golesorkhi

HOSSEINZADEH,
THE HEAD EXECUTIONER
. . . .

Azudi lights his cigarette
—say *Doctor* Azudi!
  and *Doctor* Hosseinzadeh!—
he's short, with a bald head, and eyes uneasy
as the asshole of a nervous rooster
he is a man of great renown:
he always stubs his cigarette on the back of a human hand
he never smokes more than forty a day
and the first caress is always
the privilege of this *Pahlavi* slut
and the last caress too
between the two cuffs
Azudi and Rassuli and Shadi and Manuchehri
Azudi and Parvizkhan and Rezavan and Hosseini nurse
 the patient
one extracts his nails
another his teeth
a third scours the skin
a fourth provides the shock treatment
a fifth the reflagellation
and the sixth prepares the ailing for the *coup de grace*
there's a short man whose name is Ardalan
  —say *Doctor* Ardalan!—
he fucks the afflicted
man and woman are the same to him
he holds a Ph.D. in rapacity

(and you, prisoner! you try all this time to forget
the name of the half-blind man who printed that
article of yours. He has a wife, three children, a
father and a mother, and he provides for them all)

[*45*]

and then Hosseinzadeh
        —say *Doctor* Hosseinzadeh!—
administers the final cuff
the final verdict to shoot you
comes between the two caresses

THE SHAH AND HOSSEINZADEH

the Shah has granted full authority
to Hosseinzadeh

once he mustered six of us   blindfolded
we were loaded on a truck   an hour before
dawn they took us out of the city   then they
brought us back to the city   it was
as though we were traveling from one city
to another in our dreams   then we were
unloaded and bound to six iron posts
then the command of that familiar voice was heard:
squad!
attention!
prepare to fire!
fire!

all six of us pissed our pants!

they removed our blindfolds
Hosseinzadeh and Azudi stood in a corner
pissing themselves with laughter!

say *Doctor* Hosseinzadeh! and *Doctor* Azudi!

THE PARADE OF EXECUTIONERS

. . . .

Hosseinzadeh says: I am a SAVAK Executioner!
Manuchehri says: I am a SAVAK Executioner!
Rassuli says: I am a SAVAK Executioner!
Shadi says: I am a SAVAK Executioner!
Rezvan says: I am a SAVAK Executioner!
Parvizkhan says: I am a SAVAK Executioner!
Hosseini says: I am a SAVAK Executioner!

and sometimes they say:
I am Executioner for the King of Kings, the Light of the Aryans!
I am Executioner for the King of Kings, the Light of the Aryans!
I am Executioner for the King of Kings, the Light of the Aryans!
I am Executioner for the King of Kings, the Light of the Aryans!
I am Executioner for the King of Kings, the Light of the Aryans!
I am Executioner for the King of Kings, the Light of the Aryans!
I am Executioner for the King of Kings, the Light of the Aryans!

other executioners don't say this, but they are

F.M.'s AUTOBIOGRAPHY

. . . .

sir
it's not easy for me to talk to you
here in prison there's a rumor that you're
a poet   I never wrote a word of poetry in
my life   I never even read a word of poetry
but I can tell you about the life of
a laborer in which there's no poetry
if the pain in your feet permits   if you can
forget the questions you will have to answer
in an hour   if you don't fear that your brother
has been taken away   or that your mother has had
a stroke   if you can believe that your daughter
has not been seized   listen to the words of this humble
prisoner: I am nineteen years old   when I was
three my mother beat me   at six it was my father who
whipped me   I started work when I was five
when I was eight the landlord's
sixteen-year-old son tried to rape me   he did not
succeed   because after all everything has its
limit   the mulberry cannot carry the fruit
of the melon   and the ant is not made to carry
a tree   the prick of a thick-necked rich youth
who eats butter honey meat chicken and turkey
cannot dig into the ass of a working boy
who shits none of these things   but when I was
twelve the landlord succeeded in taking the
revenge of the rich bastard   my father hanged himself
he'd wanted to kill himself for years   now he
used my disgrace for his excuse   at fourteen
I threw up the bricks of the master's house alone   at fifteen
I was pushed from a rug factory to a sock factory to
a textile factory   at sixteen the leaden air of the
printing house set in my chest   I'm a typesetter
now   for three years I had typeset *Long Live the Shah*

six days ago I decided to typeset *Long Live Liberty*
they got me five days ago   they've been pulling my
nails ever since   I've forty nails   twenty of them
belong to my hands and feet   and twenty
more belong to my hands and feet in my mind
Ardalan raped me three days ago   they haven't
raped you, have they?   that's not important
Ardalan is like a copulating dog   the bite of
his teeth is still in my shoulders   there were
of course lashes slaps kicks and obscenities too
you're a poet and they say poets know
many things   tell me what I should do next
what they will do next   pardon me for this headache
I've given you   well   what can we do after all
it's a laborer's life

someone should tell us what to do[1]

A SERMON

. . . .

when you have stopped killing us
when our feet no longer dangle from the gallows
when blindfolded eyes no longer face firing squads
what will you do my honored executioners?
                my honored executioners?
                my honored executioners?

when you have buried us heap by heap
when we can no longer confess
when there is not a nail tooth foot or hand to treat
what will you do my honored executioners?
                my honored executioners?
                my honored executioners?

a man's true vision of life and future is lost
when he thinks of you   facing you he goes
dry like a flower that suddenly wilts
tell us when we are gone and you live on
what will you do my honored executioners?
                my honored executioners?
                my honored executioners?

SEYYED ALI'S STORY

. . . .

Seyyed Ali says: As soon as they locked me in I said,
  "Long live the Shah!"
Seyyed Ali says this, and laughs

—Why did you say, "Long live the Shah!" Seyyed Ali? Why
  did you say it?

—I thought they would release me! I thought they would
  release me!

—Why didn't they release you, Seyyed Ali?

—They said, You should have said it outside! You should have
  said, "Long live the Shah of Shahs!" out there!

—Why didn't you say it out there, Seyyed Ali? What was
  wrong with saying it outside, Seyyed Ali?

—It would be a blasphemy, after all! A disgrace! How could
  you say, "Long live the Shah!" out there? One has one's
  friends, one has one's enemies. . .

—Then why did you say it here, why did you say it in prison,
  Seyyed Ali?

—I thought they would release me! I thought they would
  release me!

—What did they do?

—They beat me, all six of them. All six of them said, We shit in
  the mouth of whoever says "Long live the Shah!" in here!
  Why didn't you say it outside, you son of a bitch? Why
  didn't you say it out there?

—You should have gone outside and said it. Outside, outside, outside. . .

—No, impossible! No, no, it's a scandal to say it out there, it's disgusting, it's filthy! One has one's friends, one has one's enemies; one's friends, one's enemies. . .

TORTURE CHAMBERS
· · · · · · · · · · ·

torture chambers resemble brokers'
shops   beware! brother, beware!
if they remove the blindfold, shut your
eyes, and when you open them again,
beware! brother, beware!

whips woven of wire dangle
from huge spikes   an iron bed is a Persian
dinner cloth on which you will be set
like steaming hot food   a set of bunks
stand opposite for the instrument that will
bake your ass   the shock device is an
appendage to be plugged to a robot
the electric baton is the stiff prick
of a stallion on top of which two
scorpions sit side by side   one man
ties your feet to the bed, the other your
hands   and Azudi sits beside you with a fist
that seems to be blood and bone forged
in the spitting fat of hell
those who scourge you are men
you could only believe in your dreams
they are the only real royalists   apes
whose baby fat still rolls from their
triple chins   the stink between their legs
even months after, even in your dreams
makes you puke   another piece of furniture
is like a royal throne on which you sit
they clap your arms and legs in iron   you
resemble Lincoln's sitting statue   the nail-
pulling begins right here   there is an executioner
whose name is Shadi (happiness); he calls himself
Dr. Shadi   you know very well that there is no
happiness in him   nor is he a doctor   he

[54]

has a broad face, relatively pretty, only
the bags under the eyes cast a shade
of ugliness on the face   he's exacting
disciplined and pitiless like a pair of scales
he pulls the nails in the cool manner of
a manicurist   there is someone called Rassuli
who commonly calls himself Doctor—a toad
standing upright through the grace of God—
he has a tooth missing—a prisoner's fist must
have shattered it to pieces—he succeeds in hiding
the gap with his mustache   there is also a curious
device, made to put pressure on your skull
bit by bit the pressure is increased
does an egg confess before it's cracked?
ask our eminent surgeon, Dr. Rassuli   there is also
a handcuff whose name everybody knows
—*Dastband-e qapani*[1]—that hangs from your
manacled wrists like an anchor   you keep hanging
from it taut   as if your boat had moored in hell
there is also a time when they hang you
upside down   you retch your heart like a too big
morsel for your mouth on the floor of the torture
chamber   then a Royalist flays your legs with
a pipe   just as a *hammal*[2] wallops dust from a rug
and all this happens when the Persian
press vomit White Revolution day and night
every month they torture 2000 people
in Qizilqal'a, Committee, Evin[3] and the
dungeons of the provinces.

I tell you all this in my humble style
know that I testify: in Iran the bowels
of the earth await your pleasure   and the
gates of hell open their mouths wide as the oil
pipelines   the lines lead to those
brokers' chambers

beware! brother, beware! if they remove
the blindfold, shut your eyes, and when you
open them again, beware! brother, beware!

BARBECUE

. . . .

—would the man whose buttocks are roasted like to sit down?

—no, never! I would rather die than sit down!

he sleeps on his heart and on his knees
he arches his back
and purrs with pain
the pus and blood stick his ass to his shorts and to his pants

—doesn't the man whose back is burnt want to undress?

—no, never! I'd rather die than undress! They undressed
    me once! Isn't that enough? In a quarter of an hour you
    could roast a cow on that bed!
    I burn, burn, burn, burn forever!

I lift him under his knees
I lift him on my back
from my back his hands grip my arms
I shout behind the door
    Guard! Seventeen! Toilet!
        Guard! Guard!
slowly the cool guard comes from right or from left
with cold theatrics he throws the door open
the smell of burning nauseates him
my load is heavy but I have to run to run
crying and groaning behind my back he pulls down his pants
    pulls down his shorts
crying groaning moaning he shits as he stands

he'd rather die than sit
    or wipe himself
we return the way we came

the reek of roasting fills his mind
he's disgusted by meat
he says it's as if I was roasted
   barbecued
when I see cooked meat
I say that's me
  roasted
    barbecued

METAMORPHOSIS
. . . .

it takes only 3 hours to change a man

the delicate bloom of a student
whose eyes shone with joy
becomes a clubbed
starved prostrate cur

Azudi's red eye laughs Azudi's red eye
his teeth are so yellow
as if he had drunk a whole bowl of shit

the student's hands tremble   I had
told him, you will come back
prostrate, you will come back prostrate
I've done nothing, he had said, they won't torture me

on his knees, on his toes, on his
elbows, he comes, prostrate   it takes him
half an hour from the ward door to the cell

I told him so I told him
the guard says, whoever eats melon
should know about its slippery skin

when the door has opened and shut, the prisoner
whispers, I haven't confessed yet, I
haven't confessed

Azudi's red eye laughs Azudi's red eye
his teeth are so yellow
as if he had drunk a whole bowl of shit

it takes only 3 hours to change a man

MAMAD ALI'S HOUR

· · · · · · · · · · · ·

4 A.M. will always be a special time for Mamad Ali

(I have heard him scream I have heard him scream)

how many hours does he have in 24?
20 hours he has
he's tortured 20 hours every 24

for the remaining 4 hours
he crawls on his stomach to the cell for an hour
he stares 2 hours at the wall
he dozes off an hour
until the strident clang of the cell door
snaps him out of his sleep like the lash

it is 4 A.M.
outside
the call for morning prayer has surely begun
Dr. Rassuli is praying
then he rolls up his sleeves and takes
Mamad Ali to the torture chamber
for the sake of the god he alone knows

Mamad Ali pisses blood for days, does Mamad Ali

4 A.M. will always be a special time for Mamad Ali

(I have heard him scream I have heard him scream)

A TWENTIETH-CENTURY
PERCENTAGE
. . . .

our military courts
are like roadside inns
the wayfarer eats what he finds
the innkeeper takes what he can

in this court the accused
is in a similar fix
to stay alive
he accepts eight years in prison
for reading a forbidden book

the only thing that matters is to live
and deny death at whatever cost
and spend whatever years remain
after prison
under a summer sun
to embrace a brother who
neither remembers nor loves you
to visit the grave of a mother who
last looked on the crescent moon
two months after your sentence
to face a father who pulls himself
to the window on lame legs
to watch you come in through the door
with a bent back
the only thing that matters is to live
and deny death at whatever cost

Mamad Ali knows all this
his smile is as ash
    left on the stub of a cigarette
he has pulled eight years of his future under him
like an old rug

and squats on them
in prison

our civilization, 2,500 years old
has given Mamad Ali
2,500 days in prison
for reading a forbidden book

and still this civilization
thinks of more and more
profitable percentages

THE UNRECOGNIZED
. . . .

how soon our friends desert us
our intimates are shot
our truest friends get prison for life
our best friends are incarcerated for years and months
and the barest acquaintances
   are those
     who pretend they don't know
       the man who's just been released

we have taken an oath
   to live without recognition
and be as distant from each other as the stars

the man who is coming toward me
   has a face familiar as the sun
once he held his soup bowl to my lips
   why shouldn't I kiss him?
once the man who just went past
   cringed by me under the blows
     of Hosseini's mace
       why shouldn't I shake his hand?

and once the girl who just walked away
   raised her scream beyond prison walls
     she had been raped
       why shouldn't I kiss her hand?

how soon our friends desert us
our intimates are shot
our truest friends get prison for life
our best friends are incarcerated for years and months
and the barest acquaintances
   are those

who pretend they don't know
   the man who's just been released

we have taken an oath
  to live without recognition
and be as distant with each other as the stars

GORKY'S *MOTHER*
. . . .

today they're hitting out right and left
it is Ashura[1]
it is Ashura
the torturers scream:
>—fuck your mother that you've read Gorky's *Mother*!
>—where did you hide the translation of *Revolution in the Revolution*?[2]
>—who was the son of a bitch who gave you *Westomania*?[3]
>—guard! guard! where the hell is the guard? take this bugger away! his sister sells her cunt!
>—shut up! shut up, I say! slut! slut! slut!
>—take this bugger away! shave him!
>—have you had your picture taken?
>—open your hand! open, I say! open it like a man! *thwuck*! *thwuck*! *thwuck*! *thwuck*!
>—tell me! tell me, where's the book of the Fedayeen?[4]
>—do you know how many years you get if you read the *Manifesto*?
>—tell me! come on, tell me! if you don't tell me I'll get up and roast your ass!

today they're hitting out right and left
it is Ashura
it is Ashura
>—fuck your mother that you've read Gorky's *Mother*!

ANSWERS TO AN INTERROGATION

· · · · · · · · · · · · · · · · · · · ·

mother's face resembles a Tibetan miniature
found in Tashkent
and sold in Chicago

father, who, having bequeathed his soul
to us, is dead and gone,
resembled a Georgian Moslem
who might have traveled the Mediterranean, a pilgrim to Mecca

if you don't believe me
he's resting in the Vadiyosslam¹ of Qum
dig him out
and read the lines on his face
—that is, if you can read hieroglyphs—
and if you can distinguish hieroglyphs from cancer

once my older brother worked in a factory
then he had to wear glasses
he looked like a little James Joyce sneaking out of Ireland
his wife wanted to kill him
after twenty years locked in battle
he was at last separated from his old sow
who was not unlike you distinguished men of the SAVAK
with this slight difference—she wanted to tear out his testicles
    with her teeth

sometimes sister tries to act Florence Nightingale
at other times, Che Guevara's sister
—if Che has a sister—
with this difference, her brother's body has not been stretched
    on a platform by a colonel yet
but, believe me, her weeping is most sincere

if you want to know something about my younger brother
I should say that he is leftist in two ways
first, he is left-handed
and second, his left testicle hangs lower than his right
he has contracted mumps twice measles thrice scarlet fever
    four times chicken pox five
and gonorrhea two thousand five hundred times
once for every glorious year of the history of Iran's
    King of Kings

of the character of my wife let it suffice to say
that she only lies to you
for the present, my daughter has an absent face
and my son—if, of course, he is born a son—
in the very first decade of his life, God willing,
will witness the fall of this magnificent kingdom of yours
and he will not even put you in prison
because you will be dead by suicide
or your friends will have put you out of your misery
—or God knows to what dark hell you will have run away

other than these, I have no family
What is the next question, please?

AN IRANIAN PEASANT
INTERROGATED

· · · · · · · · · · · · ·

Q. Can you hear a fart in a jumbo jet?
A. It has no ventilation.
—Which writes best? Parker or Continental?
—No.
—What is the average daily calorie intake for an Iranian?
—Didn't I tell you?
—Explain the twelfth principle of the Iranian Revolution.
—Eleven.
—Where is the newest steel foundry in Iran?
—I'm ashamed.
—No. Don't be ashamed. Go ahead and tell us, please.
—In between. . .in between. . .one moment, please. . .it's right
   on the tip of my tongue. . .give me the first letter and I'll
   give you the rest.
—You son of a—
—Trousers. . .in trousers. . .you see, I remembered it!
—Are you an ass that doesn't understand a thing?
—Long live the Shah of Shahs the Light of the Aryans!
—Hooray! Hooray! Hooray!

ASS POEM
. . . .

When a thick-necked agent rides your neck
and your pants are pulled down to your knees
When two rape-kings politely offer each other your ass
    saying, "You first"
One
is not reminded of long ants with
one leg broken and the other leg
unable to carry the ant
And one is not reminded of the words of his late grandmother to
learn perseverance from the ants who
run fearlessly on and on—
even if they may have lost their heads and asses—
One is not reminded of Mozaffaruddin Shah who died of a hernia
or Reza Shah who died of syphilis
One is not reminded of the blond girl
whose womb the Shah recently inflated
One is not reminded of his consumptive Aunt
One is not reminded of anything at all
Only
he sees a beast bigger than himself
piercing through the depths of his bones
and the spell of degradation is nailed into his bloody asshole
as if the order "Wanted: Dead or Alive"
was tacked on his ass
And then one addresses his mother in his mind
saying
Why
don't you pull me up the way you put me down, why?

HEART

he takes a paper bag
he takes a deep breath
he blows into the paper bag
and when he claps his hands together
his breath explodes

when the bullet tears open the heart,
the heart is an exploded envelope

and after its message has gone
the mind continues its imaginings
like a driver without his car, driving forever
like a car without a driver, traveling forever

the mind
is an old woman
whose daughters are dead
whose sons are dead
whose grandchildren and great-grandchildren are dead
the mind
is a dry tree whose roots are dead

Azudi doesn't comprehend
but Golesorkhi does

AMEN TO A GOD
WHO IS NONE BUT MAN
. . . .

Lead me forth if you can, that outside there may be sun,
stars, woman, child, wind, and moon; lead me forth if you can,
this dungeon is not fit for man, this dungeon is not fit for mice
or men; show me, from this mean window-ledge on which the
spider knits his black web, the faces of my people walking with
downcast eyes to work or home or the bazaar, floating by like
mournful weeping willows; deliver me from death, dismember-
ment, the sickness of the soul, the torment of the mind, and
the torture of the body, from the hands of executioners who do
not know a cow from a mule; deliver me so that my lungs may
be restored, so that my shoulders shed their stoop and my spine
be straight, the soles of my feet be mended and my knees bend
and unbend, that my feet run and my hands ply the oars and
my soul be swamped with happiness, that I may fall in love
again and my poetry plant its seeds in the deserts, that my
own people, purer than flowers, hear my voice, that I may kiss
their hands; deliver me that I can be in love with everyone and
cavort and dance among them; deliver me from crouching and
listening in the dark to doors being opened and shut and to
boots that land on the ribs of my friends; deliver me, deliver us,
from the purgatory of these voices and screams, deliver us from
the dreams we dream in this catacomb, from the Azudis, the
Rassulis, the Manchuehris, and the Hosseinzadehs, from these
bloodthirsty spectres bearing pistols, whips, and batons, despoil-
ing our dreams and our awakenings, from these saw-wielding
ghouls, these sons-of-bitches' brains blocked with blood, from
these pimp-procurers, these sycophants of jewelers and brokers,
these prehistoric monsters who fart the slime of their entrails in
our noses in the name of Liberty and Democracy; lead me and
my friends out of this twenty-four–hour, two thousand five
hundred-year-old delirium house; deliver us from all the
tarnished traditions, all false gods, from all these slogans more
wretched than dogs' vomit, grant me and my fellow prisoners

peace, the peace of a fresh morning in early spring, and let me lay my head on my wife's womb and listen to the sweet and mysterious movement of my own-begotten life within; grant me rebirth in his body, lift this bleak nightmare of despair from my breast, drive from my mind all gods selfish and unselfish and grant me brotherhood with men, leaves, trees, and rivers; amen to a god who is none but man.

WHAT IS POETRY?

. . . .

poetry
is a shark's fin cutting a prisoner's throat
   delicately and precisely

poetry
is the sharp teeth of a rabid wolf on the shoulders
   of a wounded doe

poetry
is the exact meaning of the earth's intestines
   when broken into the small syllables of prison cells

poetry
is a cliff where executioners hurl poets into canyons below

poetry
is not a cure but the pain of a man treading the air
between an army helicopter and the waters of Hoz-e Sultan[1]
   at 200 miles per hour

poetry
is the vertical descent of a satellite of meat
   to the salt bogs of Hoz-e Sultan

poetry
is a swamp brimming over with the corpses of epic poets

poetry
is a thousand poets shot at noon by the gate of Allah Akbar[2]
   and the Mossalah[3] of Shiraz

poetry
is the poet's fall from Tabriz Arc[4]

poetry
is the immense pressure of four hands on the back of
the poet's neck when his mouth and belly are filled
   with water and the newspaper calls it suicide

poetry
is the blindfold used by prison guards to cover the
   truth of your eyes like a metaphor

poetry
is the handcuffs which do not bind your hands
   but seal your lips

poetry
is the needle used to sew up Farrokhi's[5] lips

poetry
is the full height of Sur-e Esrafil[6] on the gallows
     and the rags of Mirza Reza-ye Kermani[7] on history's
       tall form

here in prison
poetry
is this   nothing else   nothing else

UNTIL THE END

. . . .

until the end until the end when we come
to a place where a door is called
a door and the bare wall calls itself
a bare wall

there is no word of poetry here
nothing is said of rhythm
or the rhythmless
only a savage rhythm flows here
the rhythm of the door
the door through which we'll walk out
the rhythm of the wall
the bare wall at the foot of which
we'll stand and fall
squad! fire! fire!
until the end until the end when we come

THE PRISONER'S BIOGRAPHY
BY HIS WIFE

. . . .

                              six men come
                              they ask for you
                              they take you
                              they drag you away
                                    beat you
                                    knock you to the ground
                                              the ground
                                              the ground

once in Greece it happened
and two or three times in other places

in Greece
he had to leave and be by himself somewhere
to empty his bladder or to think about a poem
the bus stopped
the tourists stepped down
from ancient stairs, behind ancient trees, beside
an ancient village, we climbed the ridge at an ancient
Greek pace   the guide said, ancient Greek poets drank
this water   this water is the spirit of Calliope
the water issued from the mountain
he gazed at the water
the water resembled the springs in the homes of Tabriz
everybody came down   I was wearing white and green
Greek slippers   and thought of myself
belonging to Persephone's season
he lingered up there   was he draining his bladder   or
drinking from that water   or thinking of a poem?
returning, they showed us where the three
roads of Oedipus met
and later at a traveler's inn—I don't remember
was it before we reached the Acropolis of Corinth or that

[76]

of Thebes we slept together as always, like poets,
virgins, prostitutes, newly matured boys,
or like birds among words hot as shoulders and hair,
hot as under breasts, the openings of lovers' bodies
then he slept naked in a Greek silence like
an ancient god newly baptized, slightly fattened on Greek cuisine
then toward the middle of the silent
Grecian night his screams rose:
no!
don't beat! don't!
don't!
I've done nothing! I've
done nothing!
I've done nothing!

he was a cat
snared in a sack of nightmares
he said:
there were six men
six men only
six men
in a red room the color of
fresh blood beating me

I took him in my arms
he slept

and once in the Imperial Capital, Teheran, it
happened on Amirabad, Tal'at Street #41, the second
floor overlooking Qizilqal-a Prison
we didn't make love on that night he said
making love is like writing poetry,
sometimes you can and sometimes you cannot
but it doesn't mean that you are not a poet or a lover
one soldier was patroling behind barbed
wire another was watching from the observation
tower and another by the prison gate
his scream, incomprehensible, like the final

neighing of a shot horse, suddenly began
his scream was so savage, nervous, that it seemed
a thousand clumsy men were blowing into trumpets
all the soldiers called out:
stop! bolting their rifles
he said:
there were six men
six men   only
six men
in a red room the color of
fresh blood   beating me

I took him in my arms
he slept

and once on a march night, we were driving
on Highway 1 in California
I was thinking of Chaloos Road   he was thinking
of the road between Astara and Ardebil saying
the forest looks like a million snakes intertwined
the narrow road resembled the shoulders of a consumptive girl
we were turned away in two or three places
he said, we'll drive until we come to an empty motel
the ocean was a thousand plates of silver
shining below the cliffs   he said, I'd love to die in the
ocean, when I die,   remember   always his wills
ended with   *remember*
the lights of the car rode over the clouds
he watched the narrow road carefully, like a six-month-old
infant watching his father's bearded face
then the lights of the motel flickered
in the depths of cloud and darkness, the lights
were a cat's fearful eyes   the man there said:
we have room   the room was large   the sound
of water on the rocks reminded him of three
people whose names I didn't know:
Rimbaud, Valèry, St. John Perse   he said,

this room looks like The Drunken Boat
I didn't know why—
he always spoke of poets as if
they were nearer to him than his hands or his parents
and the names of the poems he mentioned
sounded like wine-houses, where he had drained
glasses of Ettehadieh Vodka to the last drop
we took showers   we licked each other
clean as cats on a bed the size of a cloud
then I don't remember whether I slept
first   or he
or both of us at the same time
suddenly he woke screaming, not like himself, but
as Hyde in Jekyll's body   God!
he looked like a leper   his tongue
circled in the cage of his mouth like a tiger
he said:
there were six men
six men   only
six men
in a red room the color of
fresh blood   beating me

I took him in my arms
he slept

I didn't know the meaning of these dreams   I think if Freud
and Jung had been alive they wouldn't have known either
when I told his mother, she said he's had those dreams since
childhood, yes, since childhood   and then his mother said,
perhaps they have been realized too   when I went to see him in
prison, his brother distracted the interrogator while he himself
described it to me:
one of the six men is this interrogator
I have seen the other five in that
same red room
the color of fresh blood

I said, and then. . .?
he said, it's not important anymore
all the prisoners have had this dream
this is our collective dream
and the dream happens here

I never know what he's doing
he said his whole life led him to that red room

                                    six men come
                                    they ask for you
                                    they take you
                                    they drag you away
                                          beat you
                                          knock you to the ground
                                                    the ground
                                                    the ground

he puts his hands on mine
he says, why are your hands so cold?
his beard has become whiter   he laughs
like his mother   his brother distracts
the interrogator and he himself opens his fist
in the middle of his palm there's a green star
from which a cancerous tissue spreads
he thinks of nothing   he's sitting
like one who would sit on a train with the train having made a
slight movement to leave, but as Tolstoy says, it is not clear
which way the train will go

he says goodbye
and he doesn't go
again he says
goodbye
and this time he goes
I never say goodbye to him

[*80*]

I AM AN UNDERGROUND MAN

now I am an underground man
I will never appear on the earth again
God libraries poetry belong to the earth
my holograph holds no fantasy for children
or romance for the senile

I am the rotten well of history
they seek me, they poke me, they
curse me and, finally, they drain me
I have mortgaged my beard in the vaults of history
my deadly ink will blot out the hand
outreached to me   I am not fit for textbooks
for schools and universities
if you wish to see me, look into the pit
of an oil well from the summit of Everest
throw your matches down
so that I can set the whole world aflame

I am an underground man
my fire alone shall appear on the face of the earth

THE TWO SOUNDS OF ONE WHIP

· · · · · · · · · · · · · · · · ·

every whip that descends
has two sounds
the one the whipper hears
the other the whipped
we're the second sound of the whip
which is louder?

Nero and Reza Shah hear the first sound
we hear the second

the whipper wipes away his sweat
we too wipe away our sweat
when he starts again
we say
you can whip harder than that, sir
  we have whipped you even harder

the essential connection between
a philosopher of the Middle Ages
a professional whipper
and an officer who gives his wife to his superior
is they use three names for one:
  cuckold

you can whip harder than that, sir
  we have whipped you even harder

in Gurichai[1] sixteen people froze to death in two weeks
ten liters of oil and sixteen people
the oil pipes of Iran will explode in a dawn of tulips
  we know it

with his mother's help, a man has killed his sister
shaved the eyebrows off the corpse

[*82*]

shaved her head carefully
gone out and bought a big suitcase
packed her body in the bag
put the bag on a trolley
sat his youngest sister on the suitcase
taken the handles of the trolley
and gone down the street[2]
we are not speaking of Saigon, Palestine or Belfast
we are speaking of Teheran the Imperial Capital

you can whip harder than that, sir

when the oil wells dry you'll leave
we can't wait
the whipper wipes away his sweat
we wipe away our sweat too
he whips
we are whipped
he doesn't wait
we can't wait
between whippings
a question comes to mind
what can we do so you'll go before the oil wells dry?

you can whip harder than that, sir
    we have whipped you even harder

CRYING
. . . . . .

I remember well, yes, well
when I was sitting there, alone
and in the toilet
And
I was crying
and it was the 11th of cold December

It is difficult for me to cry in public

I said, Guard
  toilet here!
    Come and take me, guard

It was the 11th of cold December

This time the guard came a bit faster
as if he somehow knew
that the flowing of tears and bursts of sobbing would disgrace me

When he opened the door I was already running
The guard shouted after me
    Run, run, before you piss your pants
    Allah willing, you will not disgrace yourself

I said:
    There is no power
    There is neither might nor strength but in God![1]

Yesterday they took away our friend
    and killed him
It is very difficult for me to cry in public

Then I was sitting alone in the toilet
and

I was crying

It was the 11th of cold December
I remember well, yes, well

THE QUESTION
· · · · · · · · ·

How lovely you are, woman!
Especially when you come to my dreams between tortures
Of course, my heart beats faster
Whether it's because of this flowering dream
or the torture awaiting my trembling shoulders
   I don't know
I always ask myself
why wasn't I with you the moments I was not
Between tortures
this question stands before me like an
enigmatic gaze:
Will there come a time when again
by my own choice, I will be with or without you?
Then how can I think that I will not want
even for a moment, not to be away from you?

ANOTHER DREAM
. . . .

Four bicycles of fire dance around you in my dream
Have we set foot in a galaxy of kisses?
Does the surf wash up to our sides?
Has the damp hair of peris stuck to our lips?

(Don't wake him,
for God's sake don't wake him)

This dream is not mine, it cannot be
It is too beautiful to be mine:
between us there is only the distance of a single flower
you have a faun's ear between your fingers
and in the next picture you walk down the staircase of a star
The other stars break around you like bubbles
No, this dream is not mine
It is too beautiful to be mine

(Don't wake him,
for God's sake don't wake him)

Waking, he crouches in the corner of his cell for hours
he speaks without prompting:
When I leave the prison
—if I leave it
I will fear being away from my wife
I will fear being away from my friends
I will fear being away from my children
for I fear that outside is another prison

HOW LONG MUST THE GAME LAST?

until his wife came to his dream one night
her eyes
like two green seasons   fresh
                    newly grown
like two sudden seasons
like
   a poem suddenly uttered by the poet
and she said—this game   how long must it last?
since when
until when
who has won the game and who is losing

he said—know that only my feet are a little wounded
and so is my heart   a little
but there is a white wall in my mind
like burnished iron
everything else seems reasonable
one day if I have the opportunity to speak
and you the patience to hear
perhaps I will tell you

and then there was no one in his dream
his mind
      was the ruins of Oriental cities
like Balkh   Nishapur
or Rega
his mind
      was the ruins of Oriental cities

LAMENTATION
. . . .

the nightingale that taught us to sing in the ruins
the nightingale that taught us saying   woe   woe upon us
the nightingale that deflowered her own voice and began singing
the nightingale that opened the lips of being
has been murdered

a brute drunk and savage
with death papers from a bastard justice
no   a cuckold justice
has silenced the nightingale on the royal block
an ignorant squad from an ignorant tribe
has fired at the nightingale from every corner
alas   she has fallen alone to the earth
the nightingale that taught us to sing in the ruins

AHMAD AGHA'S PRISON DREAM

The Buddha sits on the bank steps. Cars and tanks pass. An
American passes. A soldier passes. A promissory note passes in
the wind. An installment passes in the gutter. A newspaper
passes. The news passes. The war passes. And war movies
pass in the wind. Capital passes quickly in front, poverty passes
behind, tired. And the bank steps pass. And the moon passes
through sleepless eyes. And the Shah and the Queen pass,
crowns brimming with blood. Fat generals resembling gourmet
chefs pass in the distance with chins protruding from rolls of
flesh, naked boil-like double chins. And a chest plastered with
medals passes through the water. Swords, gauntlets, riding
crops, rifles, mortars, machine guns, missiles—pass through the
spirit. Then those others pass: Azudi, Parvizkhan, Shadi. And
that one, the one with the bald head, yes, Hosseinzadeh, Rezvan,
and others. And the steps of the bank pass. And although the
steps of the bank pass through old filthy waters, the Buddha
sits on the steps of the bank. The Buddha doesn't pass. He
sits there alone.

NOSTALGIA
·   ·   ·   ·   ·   ·   ·   ·

Oh if a man could crawl out of here
as a snake or lizard, and go—no!
Grow wings
and take flight, fly
to a place where the world no longer resembles a dirty rumor
a place where the scorched feast of sand
stretches   To be alone without
even hands or feet, without head, without cock
to be. . .
And the sea wash him constantly
like the luminous presence of a stone, smooth
circular
the sea wash him constantly

CEMETERY

. . . .

The criminal prison autumn
has arrived outside without
our seeing its signs
If we were
in Darakeh[1] now
we could see
the cemetery of yellow leaves
And now that we are not there
we had better put
our heads on the cold tiles of the cell
and sleep until
the sound of shooting startles us
and we rush
to the hole in the cell's iron door
and if the vent is open
watch the silent caravan of the innocent
like Ardaviraf[2] who saw
pre-Islamic hell-dwellers
like Mohammed[3]
who saw post-Islamic hell-dwellers
The identity of the caravan of the innocent
will not be proven in the course of time
Future archaeologists
will remove the firing squad's last bullet
rattling in the empty skull like a peanut
and send it to the laboratory
so that at least
the geological stage of the crime
will be brought to light
And the bald scholars of the future will write
two or three dissertations connecting this peanut
to a dark prehistoric time
which is our present

BROKEN IMAGES OF DECAY

I set my watch to the pulse of my blood
I see my tribe
crawling slowly up
a damp old staircase
in a room
as wide as the world's loneliness
a decrepit old man
sits wearing the crown of sun
like a bottomless copper bowl   we
stand before him in that narcotic dream
his deferential nodding does not encourage us
we see the window   no   windows
overlooking a world empty   empty
we throw ourselves from the windows
we wheel in circles
in a prolonged eternity
like falcons caught in flight
the absolute prisoners of a painting

(the only light in this prison
is the prisoner's eyes
don't put them out   don't)

we are clutching at the world's
empty shrine   we are passing through alien mirrors
nervous camels   idly
chewing
turn their jaws toward the desert

on the neck of a swift camel a virgin is crying
she dries her tears with her veil
crying is no consolation
you my mute desert sister

(the only light in this prison
is the prisoner's eyes
don't put them out   don't)

the skin rots in the summer like parched leather
the aging leper looks like an old lion
an aging tribe like an old lion
comes stumbling and rising from the fields and the deserts
their foreheads covered with sand and dry salt   their prophets
from a long silence utterly speechless   women
come stumbling and rising with half-severed breasts
are these our mothers   fathers   and brothers?
the city is occupied by leper-kings
from Balkh   Ghaznin   Rega   Nishapur   and Shiraz
      to Tabriz
sadness like Alburz   Damavand   Alvand
      and Sahand[1]
is kneeling   watching the world
and the camel passes through the curtain of the eye so that
its hump and half the floating neck escape our vision
we have to tear open our eyes to complete the image
on the neck of a swift camel a virgin is crying
crying is no consolation
you my mute desert sister   all of this
passes through the prisoner's mind

(the only light in this prison
is the prisoner's eyes
don't put them out   don't)

the Qashqaie[2] man is riding a Qashqaie horse
in the dream of the Qashqaie man in prison   and his wife
gives birth to his son upon the Qashqaie horse
in the desert under a Qashqaie moonlight   then
the prison is filled with vultures
crying is no consolation
you my mute desert sister

[*94*]

Leyli's breasts carry the smell of aloeswood, frankincense and
ambergris through the prisoner's silent mind
the woman's teeth are the color of a small white rabbit
her feet are two six-day-old kittens   the woman's knees
pass through the mind   then the thighs
and the space in between   she stands
in the sea   the water up to her breasts
the woman is alone like the sea
and naked like the sea
honey is running down her sweetly Turkoman cheekbones
a green carpet is spread upon the sand
the woman comes and lies down
the woman wants her own man   her eyes
the color of fresh opium from ancient China
opium passes through the mind of the prisoner
the prisoner picks up a stone   hurls it as far as he can
and the sound of birds   white ducks   pass through his mind
he picks up another stone and hurls it
and squats by the woman's side
the woman says
it's good like this   it is good
your shadow on my face is good
the woman closes her eyes
then suddenly opens them
the prisoner closes his eyes

his memory rises like an inscription from the depths of time
to the surface of today's wisdom
what language must it be in which the subject
is a deer   the verb—fire   object—the forest
preposition—a woman   article—a lover
    and sitting means dancing?
all these pass like a flood over the inscription
all the native tongues of the prophets pass over the inscription
and the woman passes over the inscription   her feet
the hidden code of native tongues
the prisoner reads everything in the language of the woman's feet

he reads and then he sleeps
in his dream
he sees Hassanak[3] hanging above a city
called History   his feet rotten
Babak[4] cut to pieces at the gate of ignorance
Mansur[5] walking down from his gallows holding
his blood-soaked elbows above the prisoner's head
Mossadeq[6] in the anonymous clutches of cancer

then on the gallows he sees his own friends
a red scroll hanging over each man's chest   every man
hanging from the single-branched trees in darkness
he sees his brothers' blood running through the ditches
again the women with their half-severed breasts hanging
his innocent sisters weeping in torture
he is taken through a black corridor in his dream
he's hung above a red-hot oven   terror
makes his eyelids snap open
he sees himself in the dark corner of the prison

(the only light in this prison
is the prisoner's eyes
don't put them out   don't)

When awake he dreams
of everyone   his father washing the cart-horse   from the mane
tail and testicles of the horse clear water drips
his father talks with a fat Russian soldier of
his thin horse   his father speaks Turkish   the
Russian speaks Russian but neither his father
understands Russian nor the soldier Turkish   but the horse
watches the world as if he understood
Russian   Turkish   and even the cuneiform of
Babylonian scrolls   mother her veil on her face
arrives   a bowl of water in her veiled hand   she says
su   and father takes her water bowl saying in Turkish
su   the soldier takes her water bowl   drinks

[*96*]

after an hour or perhaps a few years   in the squares
people are herded like animals to the army busses
and trucks because
God's Shadow is returning from summer vacation   God's Shadow⁷
is waking from summer sleep   not one but hundreds of
Shadows of God wake from summer siestas   from across
    the square
some with beards and mustaches   some without beards
    and mustaches
but wearing ties   some without beards or ties
but with mustaches   Shadow after Shadow of God   a bayonet
from behind the people says   bend   a nation falls to its knees
a nation that always falls to its knees
thus night becomes longer than
eternity   then a nation
crawls slowly up the damp old staircase
and takes from an old man the
crown like a bottomless copper bowl
then throws itself down from windows overlooking loneliness
like a falcon caught in flight
the absolute prisoner of a painting
and in a prolonged eternity
wheels in circles

crying is no consolation
you my mute desert sister

the camel passes through the curtain of the eye so that
its hump and half the floating neck escape
our vision   we have to tear open our eyes to complete the image

the Qashqaie man rides. . .

(the only light in this prison
is the prisoner's eyes
don't put them out   don't)

CHRONICLES OF CRIME

I couldn't finish you
        book!
last tome of history
        book!
I couldn't finish you

above us spreads a sky of
marshes   in our mirrors a thousand daggers
gleam and flash   breasts of women are fists of blood
        book!
last tome of history
        —you the biggest crime story of all
I couldn't finish you

I am the island risen from the abyss
in the apocalypse
if my voice doesn't behead me
neither the voice nor the head is mine
book! last tome of history!
—you the biggest crime story of all
still
        unfinished

Notes

An Epic in Reverse

1. The poet's parents are Turkish-speaking Iranians.
2. A famous cemetery in Qum, a religious city to the south of Teheran.
3. New City is what the people call the red light district in Teheran.
4. The Constitutional Revolution took place from 1906 to 1911.
5. In the original Persian version these words appear in Azerbaijani Turkish.
6. An old police detective, now a SAVAK member.
7. SAVAK is an abbreviation for *Sazeman-e-Ettela'at va Amniyyat-e Keshvar*, which literally translated would mean "Organization for Intelligence and Security of the Country"; it is actually the secret police.
8. The firing range west of Teheran where prisoners are taken to be shot.

The Light of Home

1. An image from the Persian poet Forough Farrokhzad (1934–67).

The Crazy Dream of the Prisoner

1. In literal translation the torture chamber is "the room for making people walk." After the prisoner has been tortured on the bed, he is made to walk on the soles of his feet, which are lashed

and bleeding. If he were not made to walk, his blood would cease to circulate properly, making it difficult for the torturers to lash him the next day. The prisoner's feet swell and are almost benumbed. The torturers want their victim to feel all the pain they are inflicting upon him.

2. The names are aliases of actual SAVAK executioners (nobody knows their real names). Obviously the government fears the possibility of future reprisals. The reason the torturers call themselves doctors is explained in the introduction.

DOCTOR AZUDI, THE PROFESSIONAL

1. Azudi is the most horrifying name in the prisons in Iran. He has been responsible for the deaths of dozens of men and women under torture. In the SAVAK hierarchy he is an assistant of Hosseinzadeh. The latter is an assistant of Sabeti, who in turn is the most important assistant of General Nassiri. General Nassiri is second to none in Iran except the Shah himself.

ZADAN! NAZADAN!

1. *Zan* means woman; *Nazan* means don't beat; *Zadan* means to beat; *Nazadan* means not to beat.

THE DEATH OF THE POET

1. Khosrow Golesorkhi was shot along with Karamat Daneshiyan in early 1974 for the alleged attempts they and ten others had made to kidnap the Queen and the Crown Prince. Government documents published in the Persian press did not show that such an attempt had actually been made, but the government turned the trial into a TV event, trying to intimidate other activists. Instead the government's own conspiracy against intellectuals and artists was revealed to the world by Iranians living abroad. Since the government hadn't the courage to announce in the newspapers that the two men had faced firing squads, I only learned of their deaths from some of my students at the University of Teheran who happened to be police officers. Khosrow wrote poetry and literary criticism but hadn't put them in book form. He also wrote under the pen name of Damon.

2. Baluch is a tribe on the southeastern border of Iran.

3. Mowlavi is Iran's great mystic poet.

[*100*]

4. Dr. Khanlari is royal tutor and chief of the Royal Academy of Culture.

F.M.'s Autobiography

1. I actually met this laborer in prison. I have given only his initials, fearing that he might still be in prison. For other prisoners I have used their first names, which are real in most cases.

Torture Chambers

1. It's actually a handcuff that ties the two hands together with one hand turned backward on the shoulder and the other forced back by the side of the body. Not only is it very heavy and the position very uncomfortable for the victim, but sometimes a heavy weight is hung from it that makes any movement impossible for the prisoner.

2. A porter.

3. The names of three very famous prisons in Teheran. Most of the torture chambers are located in these prisons where SAVAK keeps its so-called important political prisoners. Confessions are extracted here, and the prisoner is prepared for his frame-up trial.

Gorky's *Mother*

1. Ashura is the tenth day of the month of Moharram, marking Iman Hossein's martyrdom (seventh century). It is a day of mourning and self-flagellation for Iranian Moslems.

2. By Regis Debray (New York: Grove Press, 1967).

3. Jalal Al-Ahmad's (1923–69) famous manifesto on the effects of Western values on Iranian society. It has always been suppressed by the Iranian authorities and is still considered a very valuable book by the opposition in Iran.

4. A group of urban guerrillas in Iran.

Answers to an Interrogation

1. A very famous cemetery in the religious city of Qum about 150 miles south of Teheran.

What Is Poetry?

1. A salty lake south of Teheran.

2. An ancient gate of the city of Shiraz.

3. An open place for collective prayer.

4. An ancient citadel in Tabriz, my hometown.

5. A poet of the last century who wrote poetry against Qajar monarchs, one of whom ordered his mouth sewn shut.

6. Journalist of the Constitutionalist period who was killed by a Qajar king.

7. A terrorist who shot a Qajar king and was later hanged.

The Two Sounds of One Whip

1. One of the poorest quarters of the city of Tabriz. One fourth of the whole population of the city lives in it. There are 100,000 children in this area with only one school and no hospital. This poor quarter is flanked by the apartments belonging to officers of the Iranian Army stationed at one of its large bases nearby.

2. Reference to an actual event in the streets of Teheran in the winter of 1973.

Crying

1. *La hola vala quvvata illa billah*: "There is neither might nor strength but in God," used rather ironically here, is the basis for the rhythmical pattern of the *Ruba'i* (quatrain) in Persian poetry. This foot underlies the blank verse I used in the original version of the poem.

Cemetery

1. A beautiful village to the north of Teheran.

2. The Zoroastrian priest of the Sassanid period in Iran who went to visit the Inferno and upon return wrote *Ardavirafnameh* (*The Book of Ardaviraf*).

3. The *Me'raj*, or ascension of the Prophet Mohammed, had tremendous influence on Dante's *Divine Comedy*.

Broken Images of Decay

1. Mountain ranges in Iran.

2. A great Iranian nomadic tribe, originally Turkish.

3. A minister of Sultan Mahmoud in the tenth century, killed and dismembered later by Sulton Mas'ood.

4. Babak-e Khorramdin, the great Azerbaijani rebel who revolted against the caliph but later was defeated and caught. His body was cut into three pieces and hung in the city of Baghdad.

5. Mansur Al-Hallaj, the great mystic, who was dismembered in Baghdad in the tenth century.

6. Premier of Iran, deposed by a CIA coup in 1953, when the present Shah started his dictatorship.

7. God's Shadow is a literal translation of the Arabic word combination *Zillullah*. It is a title the Iranian kings have used for centuries in order to give their rule a metaphysical backing. The present monarch also calls himself God's Shadow.

This collection of poems, savage and tender by turns, introduces to the English-speaking world an outstanding Iranian poet and critic (now in exile in the United States). Originally composed in Persian and now translated into English by the poet himself, the forty-one poems included in *God's Shadow* are haunting and disturbing reflections on the author's arrest by the Iranian secret police (SAVAK) early in the fall of 1973 and his detention for a period of 102 days. The precise grounds for Baraheni's imprisonment were never specified, but his political views, which were—and remain—highly critical of the government of Iran, appear to have been behind it. Baraheni's release in December 1973 came as abruptly as his arrest, and he attributes it to efforts exerted by writers in Europe and in America.

God's Shadow deals unsparingly with prison life—with the torture, beatings, and homosexual rape that were a part of the fabric of daily existence—and the force of these poems unquestionably derives in part from the author's political conviction, strengthened under the stimulus of oppression. But ultimately the poems succeed because they are powerful expressions of an individual voice, beautifully rendered into English in a rare collaboration between an author and himself as translator.